Giving the Best in Worship is a book that I've wanted to write for a number of years. Coming from a comparatively traditional background, I've had to unlearn and reappraise some of my attitudes to appreciate the real potential of worship — not that I've abandoned all that I've been accustomed to. Far from it! But the wind of the Holy Spirit has blown through my life and as I've meditated on Scripture and applied what I've discovered, so worship has become more meaningful.

I do need to remind you that this handbook is not intended to be an all-comprehensive insight into the great tenets of our faith! You'll certainly find that it has theological integrity, and it is written to help individuals and groups understand what the Bible has to teach on the subject of worship.

Groups using this material will find it valuable to prepare by reading a section through before coming together. Group leaders, of course, should seek to familiarise themselves thoroughly with each chapter, and work through the practical exercises in anticipation of leading lively discussion. The various questions and discussion points will be useful for group and individual Bible study. But above all, I hope that it will make you more aware of the power in praise.

I share the leadership in a team ministry and one of my well-used expressions that I pass on to our ministry teams has been quoted back at me time and time again. "You will never get your work right until you get your worship right!" By that, I mean that effective service is rooted in a heart that is overflowing with love for the Lord.

I firmly believe that is true, for until we recognise afresh the sovereignty and majesty of God, and the immensity of His love for us, then we shall never be motivated to serve Him. Instruction and teaching can never be a substitute for love and devotion.

I've also included a section that I hope will be of use to worship leaders. The danger of my assuming the right to address this issue is that people assume that there are experts who lead worship and bring a touch of the "heavenlies" to all that they do. My suggestions are made out of a learning experience that continues to teach me new things, so I hope that it will be of valuable use to those of you who are still struggling in the "earthlies".

I hope that you will be encouraged as you use this guide, and that the instruction and practical exercises will lead you into a deeper appreciation of the greatness of God. May your investment in time and study bring great joy in heaven and excitement on earth!

Dave Pope

1

Worship?

THE AIM OF WORSHIP

Our aim in worship is to please God — nothing more and nothing less. A rather simplistic definition perhaps, but one that is nevertheless fundamental and basic to our understanding of this subject.

Our aim in worship — and I say this carefully — is to put a smile on God's face. To give Him pleasure and joy as He sees His children giving Him His rightful place in their lives.

The writer to the Hebrews uses the phrase "sacrifice of praise" (Hebrews 13:15). Does that strike you as being strange? Sometimes we take the opportunity for praise and worship so lightly that we lose sight of the fact that worship should cost us something!

When wise men came to bring their adoration to the infant King, they presented themselves in humility and gave valuable presents to emphasise their worship. "They bowed down and worshipped him. Then they opened their treasures and presented him with gifts of gold and of incense and of myrrh" (Matthew 2:11).

Yet so often, we fail to embody this perspective in our worship. Sacrifice implies giving something that is costly — self-denial, tithes and offerings, obedience and total commitment in our lifestyle. Of course, one of the glorious "by-products" of God-honouring worship is the encouragement of the worshipper.

The Bible tells us that God is "the praise of Israel" (Psalm 22:3). As we bless the Lord in our worship, so by His Spirit He lifts our hearts and reminds us that we are His children. We please Him when we confess our sin, when we repent, when we ask for forgiveness, and He blesses us when we walk more closely to Him. God is glorified when we worship Him with every fibre of our being, in what we do and not just in what we say. True worship always comes from the heart, not just from the lips.

For many years, a very famous painting hung in the National Gallery in a European city; people travelled from far and wide to view this great work of art. After some years had passed by, it was time to clean and restore the picture, and as the craftsmen began their work, something quite remarkable happened. The surface paint began to flake away, revealing another picture that had been originally painted onto the canvas.

As restoration proceeded, it was soon discovered — to the great embarrassment of the gallery — that the real masterpiece had been hidden for hundreds of years and that people had been viewing a "mask", rather than the real work of art.

In our study of worship, I want us to remove the superficial ideas that abound today and get back to the original. Too many of us hold to anaemic views and ideas that have taken the heart out of worship.

In our culture, we seem to have a remarkable way of devaluing our vocabulary, and the word "worship" has come under this pressure. Sometimes it has happened as a result of wrong associations, but more often than not, it is a consequence of inadequate teaching and we can be spiritually much the poorer for it. A.W. Tozer, in one of his writings, describes worship as "the missing jewel of the evangelical church"[1] — let's discover its true value.

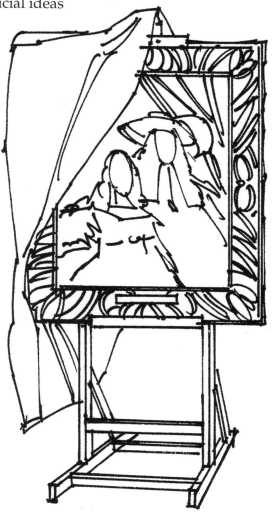

The word "worship" in the English language is a derivative of an Anglo-Saxon word *wercscipe*, which simply means "to appreciate the worth of". It is used to express value that is placed on an object or a person. Therefore when we worship something or someone, we lavish our love, attention and praise in that particular direction, whether it be our wife, our children, a close friend, or even a car! So when we talk of worshipping God, we imply that we are *appreciating His worth in all that we do in order to communicate our love for Him.*

THE BIBLE AND WORSHIP

When we turn to Scripture, worship is inherent in all that we read. The first few chapters of Genesis give us an insight into God's magnificent plan and purpose in creation when He made the universe in which we live and He saw that it was good. His creative genius reached its pinnacle in the creation of human life — Adam and Eve, created by God to enjoy the good things God had provided. He created them to give Him pleasure. But it all went terribly wrong and as man disobeyed his Creator, so evil came into the world. The die was cast and God became displeased.

As the Old Testament unfolds, God's nature and character come to the fore. He is the God of nations — all powerful and truly mighty — a holy God who commands His people to worship Him. "Fear the Lord your God, serve him only and take your oaths in his name" (Deuteronomy 6:13).

Out of history and into poetry; the Psalms describe the riches of God and reveal the Psalmist's desire to worship the Lord with praise and all that is within him.

From poetry to prophecy — an insight into God's judgment on disobedience and the "fickleness" of the human spirit.

Then on into the New Testament where a new pattern of worship emerges. The traditions of Old Testament worship are threatened by the phenomenal growth of the early Christian church, and although the New Testament Christians still maintained links with the Temple and the Synagogue, there were other factors to be considered.

Persecution drove Christians out of the traditional worship places, and the addition of Gentile believers meant they would not be able to visit the Temple; Gentiles were uncircumcised so they would have no place in the Temple.

The outpouring of the Holy Spirit on the day of Pentecost (as prophesied in Joel 2:28–32), the day of the new covenant foretold by Jeremiah and accompanied by Christ's death on the cross — the final sacrifice — heralded a new basis for worship.

Jesus, now our High Priest, marks the dawn of a new era and the Book of Revelation gives a climactic insight into worship in the heavenlies: a magnificent, awesome gathering of angels and saints giving Jesus His rightful place at the centre of praise and worship.

So much for what I call a "helicopteric" view of worship as shown in Scripture. We now need to land the helicopter; to move from the general overview to more particular areas, in order to understand what the Old and New Testaments teach us about principles and practices in worship.

From what you have learned so far, give your own definition of worship.

Worship is _____

_____

_____

" . . . great is the Lord and most worthy of praise . . . ascribe to the Lord the glory due to his name."

1 Chronicles 16:25, 29

WORSHIP IN THE OLD TESTAMENT

Let's turn to the book of Exodus:

> "But if the servant declares, 'love my master and my wife and children and do not want to go free,' then his master must take him before the judges. He shall take him to the door or the door-post and pierce his ear with an awl. Then he will be his servant for life." (Exodus 21:5, 6)

An interesting custom to say the least, but one which teaches us something of the dynamic of worship from Hebrew tradition. The word *abodah* describes the service that is provided by a slave to his master. A slave in Old Testament times was totally subject to his master, available to serve and perform duties as his master decreed.

However, the ideal relationship was where a slave fulfilled his service — not because he was under orders, but because he loved his master and delighted to serve him. So, when according to custom a slave was released after six years of service, he could forfeit this right and offer to continue service as a labour of love.

Then followed the ceremony described in Exodus 21. This is a beautiful picture of total commitment, and indeed, spiritual worship — the worshipping servant with a heart full of love for his master.

The second Hebrew word that is important to notice is *shachah* which means "to bow down". Thus, "When Abraham's servant heard what they said, he bowed down to the ground before the Lord" (Genesis 24:52). And when the glory of God filled the Temple of Solomon, the Israelites "knelt on the pavement with their faces to the ground, and they worshipped and gave thanks to the Lord" (2 Chronicles 7:3).

THINK . . .

What is the parallel between our relationship with God and that of the servant and master in Exodus 21:5,6?

How might this affect our attitude in worship?

"At the very heart of Biblical worship is this attitude of humble submission and reverence. There are other elements such as praise and thanksgiving and at times exuberant joy. But always there is the underlying attitude of awe and humility. The worshipper may come with confidence to God. He may present his needs with the assurance that the Lord hears. But he is always the obedient servant before his master, with his spirit bowed in adoring submission before the Lord of hosts."

Herbert Carson [2]

The Old Testament pattern of worship is built on the principle of sacrifice. Before a burnt offering could be made, which was the symbol of a man's total commitment, he presented a sin offering to receive forgiveness where the sacrifice was the penalty-bearing substitute.

But there was also an emphasis on inner integrity, not simply on the offering of sacrifice, hence that searching question to be found in Micah:

> "With what shall I come before the Lord and bow down before the exalted God? Shall I come before him with burnt offerings, with calves a year old? Will the Lord be pleased with thousands of rams, with ten thousand rivers of oil? Shall I offer my firstborn for my transgression, the fruit of my body for the sin of my soul?" (Micah 6:6–8)

David's Psalms express the joy of inner peace through repentance and consistency in lifestyle. His songs are full of that exuberant praise that reflects a heart overflowing with delight.

Read Psalm 103.

What fills David's heart with praise?

List his reasons for praising God:

_____

_____

_____

_____

_____

The prophets only serve to underline the importance of integrity in worship. Isaiah is quick to vent his anger on Judah because of their idolatry.

> " 'The multitude of your sacrifices — what are they to me?' says the Lord. 'I have more than enough of burnt offerings, of rams and the fat of fattened animals; I have no pleasure in the blood of bulls and lambs and goats.' " (Isaiah 1:11)

And Amos waxes eloquently angry against those who perform religious ritual and yet are deliberately committing sin and flying in the face of God.

> " 'I hate, I despise your religious feasts; I cannot stand your assemblies. Even though you bring me burnt offerings and grain offerings, I will not accept them. Though you bring choice fellowship offerings, I will have no regard for them. Away with the noise of your songs! I will not listen to the music of your harps. But let justice roll on like a river, righteousness like a never-failing stream!'" (Amos 5:21–24)

These words of Amos should be allowed to reverberate through our fellowships today. It may be cultural to attend church, doing so may induce a sense of well-being, the church offering plate may provide an escape route for guilt and singing songs may be a pleasurable exercise, but to what purpose? If our hearts are cold and our lives steeped in sin, then all of this creates a foul odour in heaven — if it actually gets that far. I have a hunch that mock worship never gets further than the ceiling rafters!

The feasts and the places of worship were also highly significant. The feasts — The Feast of Unleavened Bread, The Feast of Weeks and The Feast of Tabernacles — were celebrated to remind Israel of the relationship between God and His people, and to encourage them to worship Him.

Temple worship obviously thrilled the hearts of the worshippers:

> "How lovely is your dwelling-place, O Lord Almighty! My soul yearns, even faints for the courts of the Lord; my heart and my flesh cry out for the living God. Even the sparrow has found a home, and the swallow a nest for herself, where she may have her young — a place near your altar, O Lord Almighty, my King and my God. Blessed are those who dwell in your house; they are ever praising you . . . Better is one day in your courts than a thousand elsewhere; I would rather be a doorkeeper in the house of my God than dwell in the tents of the wicked." (Psalm 84:1–4, 10)

KEY QUESTION

What was wrong with the worship described in Isaiah 1:11 and Amos 5:21–24?

Do we have any twentieth century examples that would also displease God?

8

Some have suggested that it is the tradition of Temple worship that had a profound impact on worship in the New Testament churches and provided a pattern for Christian worship. Awe, majesty, joy, psalms and songs — all woven into the New Testament praise without the ritualistic attendance to Temple duties.

The synagogue also came into being when the Temple of Jerusalem was destroyed by the Babylonians in 587 BC. As a result of the nation being scattered, so local meeting places were established. A synagogue literally means "a place of assembly" and even when the Temple was restored, these meeting places continued to exist. In the synagogue there was no altar; instead a portable ark, containing the scrolls of the law and the prophets. The reading of the law replaced sacrificial offerings. This law that was read was and is known as the *Torah* and again, the practice of worship in the synagogue proved to be of great significance for the early Christian church, with the essential ingredients of worship being praise, prayer, reading of Scripture and singing psalms.

THINK . . .

Imagine a visitor comes to your church next Sunday. Would they respond to the worship in the same way as David expressed his love for the house of God? If not, why not?

When does a worship service bring the same thrill to your heart as did Temple worship for David?

WORSHIP IN THE NEW TESTAMENT

As we turn to examine New Testament worship, we do not abandon all of the Old Testament principles. The early Christians that we discover in the opening chapters of The Acts of the Apostles were Jewish, and the traditions of the Temple and synagogue would still have been adhered to.

But there were changes, and what with the influx of non-Jewish believers and subsequent alienation and persecution, the character of the church and the practice of worship began to create divergence from the Jewish traditions.

The established meeting places were supplemented by fellowships that were planted as a result of persecution and opposition from the Jewish leaders, but perhaps the most significant factor in the development of New Testament worship was the outpouring of the Holy Spirit.

When He came, He provided the fulfilment of Old Testament prophecy and sealed the transition to a more embracing fellowship of believers. As Peter declared,

> "This is what was spoken by the prophet Joel: 'In the last days, God says, "I will pour out my Spirit on all people. Your sons and daughters will prophesy, your young men will see visions, your old men will dream dreams." ' " (Acts 2:16,17)

Herbert Carson describes this most succinctly:

> "The day of the New Covenant had now come. The Messiah had accomplished His ministry, offered the final sacrifice which abrogated all lesser sacrifices and was now exalted as the one, all-sufficient, High Priest. As a result, the doors were opened, not only to Jews but also to Gentiles.
>
> The Gospel age had dawned and new principles were needed for the men and women of this new age. There were principles embodying the ageless truths inherited from the prophets, but also declaring the New Life in the Spirit which is a hallmark of New Testament Christianity." [3]

There were many principles in worship that remained the same — the centrality of Scripture and the glory of God taking pride of place. Paul always showed a great concern when worship became "man-orientated" (Colossians 2:23) and indeed, alongside these fundamental principles, the New Testament emphasises the importance of order in worship.

However, within this pattern, scope was also given for the development of ministries and gifting, as long as the end result was the glory of God and the edification of the church. Freedom must never become an excuse for licence; and with the exercise of spiritual gifts, and the scope given for individual and corporate expression, Paul was anxious to make sure that the church was built up and not torn apart. Perhaps we need a fresh understanding of this today.

It was important that the congregation should understand what was happening in worship, particularly as believers were drawn from many backgrounds and had varying needs. Hence Paul's insistence that the gift of tongues should always be interpreted, and that prophecy be exercised and made intelligible for the whole fellowship. Confusion has never been the best mortar for building the Kingdom!

Prayer and praise were particularly emphasised. Christians were not only encouraged to pray as individuals, but also to be involved in corporate prayer and it has already been emphasised that praise percolates through the drama of the New Testament.

I never cease to be amazed at how often suffering and pain prove to be the springboard of praise. As the pressure became greater, the praise became more potent and enthusiastic. I wonder if our worship today would take the same course if our freedom as believers was removed?

Can you think of any ways in which worship might be a sacrifice of praise?

Can you give any examples from your own experience?

_____

_____

_____

_____

Let's look at more specific definitions. The most popular Greek word used in the New Testament to describe worship is *proskyneo*. This word is used 49 times and its meaning is *to come towards, to kiss the hand*[4] and denotes both the external act of prostrating oneself in worship and the corresponding inward attitude of reverence and humility.

This is wonderfully illustrated in the New Testament time and time again, but perfectly in the book of John when Jesus is talking to the lady of Samaria. "God is spirit, and his worshippers must worship in spirit and in truth." (John 4:24)

Graham Kendrick in his book *Worship* comments,

> "This gives us a beautiful picture of worship as we approach the King of kings and Lord of lords; with open face eye to eye, our hearts full of love and thanks, our will set firmly to obey Him, enjoying an intimacy and a mutual affection that the watching angels find astounding."[5]

The other word used in the New Testament for worship is *latreuontes* — a word appearing 26 times which, simply translated, means *service*. It is often used for public worship as in Paul's letter to the Philippians. "For it is we who are the circumcision, we who worship by the Spirit of God, who glory in Christ Jesus, and who put no confidence in the flesh" (Philippians 3:3).

This is the emphasis of New Testament worship, providing the life-blood to all that Paul and other New Testament writers had to say about conduct, practicalities, gifts, holiness, prayer, praise, warfare and unity. Lose this perspective of reverence and service and you lose the heart of what worship really is.

And yet it is important to realise that the early church often got it wrong! What an encouragement — if I dare say that — to those of us who are often embroiled in discussions and arguments in today's church.

Acts 2 may give us some of the excitement, but Paul's letters to the Corinthians probably shows us something of his exasperation with the immaturity, carnality and double standards that existed at that time. Of course, there has never been a perfect church, and there never will be, while the likes of you and I make up its numbers.

What inspires you to worship God?

Look at Psalm 145. David praises God because of His character, for who He is, not just because of what He has done.

What aspects of God's character can you identify in the psalm?

_____   _____

_____   _____

_____   _____

_____   _____

2

I recently installed in my garden a waterfall which runs into a pool stocked with goldfish and Koi carp. One day in the middle of summer the water level of the pool dropped dramatically — to the extent that the fish were floundering in the shallow water amongst all the weeds and debris.

Closer examination revealed the problem. A jam jar had fallen into the watercourse, obstructing one of the channels, and the flow of water had been diverted over the side of the rocks and into the soil. The water had almost drained away, with near catastrophic results for the welfare of the fish!

Worship that honours God flows from a life that is open and in tune with Him, but there are times when we allow all kinds of things to obstruct and hinder that. Some folks seem to think that worship happens the moment the minister announces the first hymn on a Sunday morning. An honest appraisal of what constitutes real worship places the responsibility firmly on us as individuals — not on a style of worship or a particular leader.

We therefore must be prepared to examine our hearts before a holy God and identify those things which would hinder or prevent us bringing a praise offering to the Lord.

Such questions as "Is my attitude wrong today?", "What am I expecting God to do this morning?" and "What am I prepared to give to Him today?" all demand honest answers if we are to be clean and open channels for worship to flow.

> **THINK . . .**
> What are the potential blockages in our lives which can hinder worship?

HINDRANCES

1. Selfishness

"Didn't get much out of the service this morning." "Thought the hymns were boring." "Vicar seemed to be rambling in his sermon tonight — it was a waste of time being there." How often have we made similar comments after attending a worship service at our local church? Instead of the Sunday joint, we end up with roast preacher for lunch! It's very easy to be critical and far more difficult to be constructive, but this is mainly due to a wrong appraisal of what worship is all about.

We don't share in praise and worship essentially to get something out of it — that is entirely selfish. Our intention should be to give to the Lord out of the very best that we have — our devotion, enthusiasm, attention — worship that unequivocally lifts up His name. It's a precious benefit of inspired worship that the worshipper gets blessed, but that is not our prime motivation.

It is in the very nature of man to want to receive blessing rather than to give. Recently I preached on Psalm 37:4, "Delight yourself in the Lord and He will give you the desires of your heart."

Just before the meeting I was asked for the text and I quoted the reference. "Wonderful verse," came the reply, " 'He will give you the desires of your heart.'" In a polite way I pointed out the incompleteness of that quotation, but do you see the emphasis that came through here? We often want to take the blessing without the responsibility, which in this case means delighting in the Lord. First things first if our worship is to be unhindered.

Think of ways whereby you can delight yourself in the Lord. Be as practical as possible. Set aside ten minutes every day next week to concentrate on "delighting yourself" in the Lord — and jot down a thought, Bible verse or song which seems most appropriate that day:

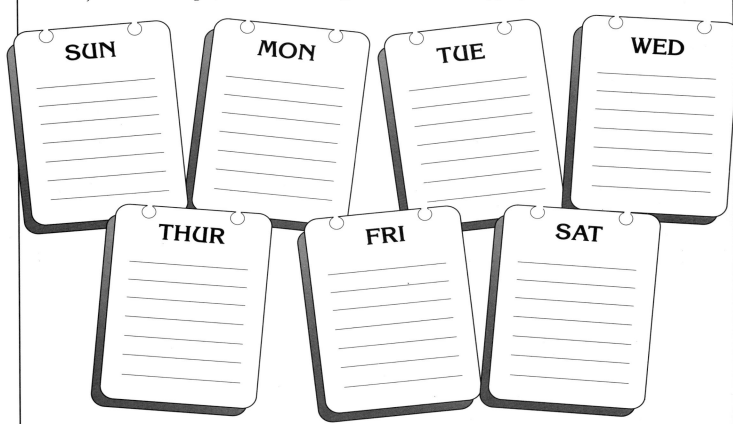

2. Familiarity

On one occasion Jesus returned to His home town and "He did not do many miracles there because of their lack of faith" (Matthew 13:58). This possibly startling incident illustrates very closely that God is actually inhibited when His people expect very little.

The point has already been made that worship is about giving to God, but it is worth asking the question whether we actually expect God to be present when we come together to worship Him.

It is easy to become so familiar with the time and place, even the format, the hymns and the people, that it all becomes safe and predictable.

Familiarity encourages stagnation. The danger is that some of our services might run just as efficiently even if God, by His Spirit, was not in attendance!

Worship should emphasise the living, vibrant character of the God we honour, and yet so often there is that sense of inertness and staleness about what we do.

In Psalm 62:5, David reminds us to base our expectation in God above:

"Find rest, O my soul, in God alone;
my hope comes from him.
He alone is my rock and my salvation;
he is my fortress, I shall not be shaken."

Why do you think that expectation is important in worship?

1 _____

2 _____

3 _____

3. Fear

God is a dynamic God and the *Oxford English Dictionary* describes dynamic as "full of energy, full of life". R.T. Kendall, in his book *Worshipping God* quotes Jonathan Edwards when he says that, "the task of every nation is to discover in which direction the Sovereign Redeemer is moving and then to move in that direction."[1]

Dr Kendall continues, "Dynamic worship is worship by the Spirit of God, and we will know that the Spirit is present if three things follow: an increase of faith, of fellowship and of freedom." But is it not true to say that too often fear holds many back from moving on into all that God wants to show us?

Of course there have been excesses in worship and in some instances things have gone desperately wrong, but we must never allow the faults of others to hinder us from moving on into a deeper expression and appreciation of God.

Paul reminds us "Where the Spirit of the Lord is, there is freedom" (2 Corinthians 3:17). Yes, some have changed "freedom" into "licence", but let us not keep looking over our shoulders — we need to look unto Jesus.

I don't want to play down the desperate means the devil has used to wreak havoc in this area, but it really is no different to New Testament times. After all, the devil can only counterfeit that which is original so that in itself should inspire us to move on into greater things. "Perfect love casts out fear" (1 John 4:18) — and although this was not written specifically in the context of worship, the same principle applies.

4. Boredom

Perhaps you remember the children's nursery rhyme,

> " 'Pussycat, Pussycat, where have you been?' 'I've been up to London to visit the Queen.' 'Pussycat, Pussycat, what did you there?' 'I frightened a little mouse under the chair.' "

Now, before you think you picked up the wrong book by mistake, take a second look at this rhyme. It may not make an obvious theological statement — or does it?!! Imagine being invited to London to visit the Queen and all you end up doing is frightening mice around Buckingham Palace!

Far fetched maybe, but what do we often do when we are summoned into the presence of the King of kings? Count how many people are wearing red hats? Guess how many pipes are on the organ? Figure out how many pieces of stained glass are in the window?

The onus of course is on leadership and laity alike to make sure that the variety in worship mirrors the great variety in the character of God. But let's not forget one important fact — we worship God for who He is, not simply because of what He has done. His character is so impressive, outside of His sovereign acts of mercy and grace, that focussing on Him should ensure that boredom does not creep into our worship agenda.

"I rejoiced with those who said to me, 'Let us go to the house of the Lord.' "

Psalm 122:1

Complete the following:

I look forward to going to church because

1 _____

2 _____

3 _____

4 _____

5 _____

5. No Personal Relationship With God

The only people who can truly worship God are those who are born again by the Spirit of God. Paul reminds us in his letter to the Romans, "through Christ Jesus the law of the Spirit of life set me free from the law of sin and death" (Romans 8:2).

The unbeliever may go through some form of worship, but it is not true worship. Until the law of the Spirit has brought release through salvation, worship can only be a form of godliness.

Sadly, however, this is the case in many of our churches today where people attend because it is the British tradition or because they like the music or because the family have always had connections with the church. They are unable to enjoy true worship because the Spirit of Christ has not brought real life to their spirit. But it could be theirs for the asking.

6. Stale Relationship with God

What of the individual whose experience of the Lord has become stale? The flames of love and devotion are now but dying embers. No wonder that worship becomes an uphill struggle!

If God is moving His people on and some dig their heels in *en route*, it is hardly surprising that their hearts are not warmed by an atmosphere of praise.

Just as any relationship needs cultivation and attention, so it is in our walk with the Lord. There is no greater test of faithfulness than the litmus paper of worship.

Identify some of the factors that help and hinder you in worship.

I find worship difficult because

1. _____

2. _____

3. _____

4. _____

5. _____

I am helped in worship by

1. _____

2. _____

3. _____

4. _____

5. _____

Ask yourself what things make you feel cautious or fearful in worship? Put into order of importance the following comments, adding any others of personal concern:

☐ Awareness of what other people might think.

☐ Becoming over emotional

☐ Awareness of ways in which I have let God down.

☐ Feeling insecure when I don't know the songs.

☐ That God might speak to me in worship and challenge me about my lifestyle.

☐ How do I know if I am responding to God or to peer pressure?

☐ Feeling unsure of how much God loves me.

☐ _____

☐ _____

Get into pairs, and together pray through your list of "blockages" asking God to help you worship Him in spirit and in truth.

HOW WE WORSHIP

With all the interest generated in worship in recent years, it is easy to fall into the trap of thinking that worship activity is primarily concerned with hymns and Sunday services. But worship is not what we do, it is what we are!

Hands raised in worship on a Sunday, but found to be meddling in dubious activity on a Monday, add nothing to worship integrity.

It's time to recognise the broader implications of delighting God our Creator. Many would generate more heat than light discussing differences in worship styles instead of being more diligent in the way they behave.

In Romans 12:1 Paul writes: "I urge you, brothers, in view of God's mercy, to

_____

_____

this is your spiritual act of worship" (Romans 12:1).

Worship is not about what we do on a Sunday morning between 10:30 am and 12:00 noon. We worship and honour God by the manner in which we live our lives — by our behaviour, our attitudes, our conversation and our character.

> "He is no fool who gives up what he cannot keep to gain what he can never lose."
>
> Jim Elliott

"Living sacrifices" — the phrase used by the Apostle Paul — takes us back to the section when we examined Old Testament traditions, but the implication here is that God wants a sacrifice that is expensive to us and pleasing to Him. What He wants is nothing more and nothing less than total commitment, seven days per week, twelve months in the year. Who was it that said that the trouble with living sacrifices is that they have a tendency to creep off the altar!

Turn to James Chapter 1

James was a very practical "down to earth" fellow and in this letter, he is addressing Jews who were trying to turn the church into a middle-class society. He was concerned that religion had become pride of place and real worship, in terms of lifestyle, attitude and behaviour had been dismissed.

Read the whole of James Chapter 1 and then discuss:

Identify where the "living sacrifices" had crawled off the altar! Where had the people made mistakes?

_____

_____

_____

_____

How is James Chapter 1 applicable to the church in the Twentieth Century?

When writing to the church at Ephesus, Paul makes a similar point. "As a prisoner for the Lord, then, I urge you to live a life worthy of the calling you have received. Be completely humble and gentle; be patient, bearing with one another in love" (Ephesians 4:1,2). When we live worthy of our calling people notice.

A little while ago in the city of Bristol, there lived a General Practitioner called Dr Hiley. His son was training to be a Christian minister and he had also received a doctorate at college. One evening a knock came on the door of the house where they both lived and when a friend of the family opened the door she discovered a lady on the doorstep, asking to speak to Dr Hiley. "Very well," said the friend, "but do you want the one who preaches or the one who practices?" The point is obvious! Consistent lifestyle is the central issue in worship, when I am able to say, "I believe" and my next-door neighbour says, "He behaves."

Imagine that a reporter from the local newspaper is writing a feature on you and your lifestyle. He knows that you are a Christian and is told to follow you around for seven days. List those areas of your life which would be the most confusing for him to understand? Then in column B write down how you would try to explain it to him — or apologise!

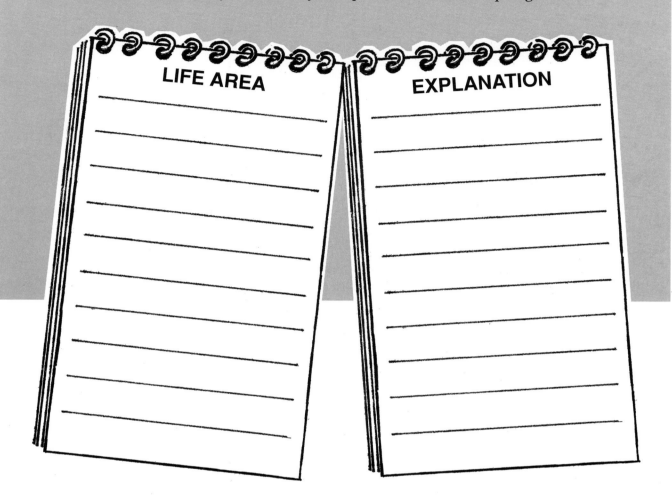

LIFE AREA

EXPLANATION

LET'S SING

Singing songs has always been an integral feature of worship, making a first Biblical appearance in Exodus, chapter 15. Israel had just experienced God's anger, but in His mercy God made a means of deliverance and the children of Israel burst into song.

> "I will sing to the Lord for he is highly exalted. The horse and its rider he has hurled into the sea. The Lord is my strength and my song; he has become my salvation." (Exodus 15:1,2)

Here was a thankful people, full of joy and praise as they acknowledged God's salvation.

As we turn to 1 Chronicles, we discover that singing was cultivated for worship in the Temple:

> "All these men were under the supervision of their fathers for the music of the temple of the Lord, with cymbals, lyres and harps, for the ministry at the house of God. Asaph, Jeduthun and Heman were under the supervision of the king. Along with their relatives — all of them trained and skilled in music for the Lord." (1 Chronicles 25:6, 7)

Of course the Psalms give substantial weight to the use of spiritual songs in worship: "I will sing of the Lord's great love for ever" (Psalm 89:1); "Sing joyfully to the Lord, you righteous; it is fitting for the upright to praise him" (Psalm 33:1).

As we turn to the New Testament we discover that Paul makes an interesting point when he teaches the early believers how to use songs. He says,

> "Be filled with the Spirit. Speak to one another with psalms, hymns and spiritual songs. Sing and make music in your heart to the Lord." (Ephesians 5:18,19)

Paul stresses here that the priority is to be filled with the Spirit, and that our singing stems from that indwelling power of the Lord. That's particularly helpful for those who have questioned the role of music in the church.

This is further supported by his words to the church at Colossae when he writes,

> "Let the word of Christ dwell in you richly as you teach and admonish one another with all wisdom, and as you sing psalms, hymns and spiritual songs with gratitude in your hearts to God." (Colossians 3:16)

Notice again a priority; it's not the psalm, not the song, but the word of God living in our hearts. An accurate summary from these two passages helps us in our thinking here. "Let the word of God live in you, be filled with the Spirit — and then sing to the Lord."

LET'S MAKE MUSIC

Scripture is impregnated with music. It is first mentioned at the beginning of Genesis where Jubal is introduced as the "father of all who play the harp and flute" (Genesis 4:21).

In the time of Moses, we read about the use of trumpets to bring people together: "The Lord said to Moses, 'Make two trumpets of hammered silver, and use them for calling the community together and for having the camps set out' " (Numbers 10:1,2) and a little later we are introduced to Miriam, who played the tambourine.

In David's time, women increasingly played an important part in the ministry of music and David, of course, wrote and played his own compositions.

Music is a wonderful servant, but a terrible master. In recent years controversy concerning the role of music in worship and in evangelism has caused much misunderstanding. The book *Pop Goes the Gospel* [1] raised some important issues, and even though much of what it had to say was true, it was narrowly researched and has left a legacy of suspicion of Christian music and musicians.

It would, however, be right to admit that some musicians have been most unwise in their use of music — promoting self, musical skill (or lack of it!) and entertainment. But as long as we appreciate that as far as worship is concerned, music is an aid — and not an end in itself — we need to encourage its use.

Note down this summary of Paul's three-fold priority for our worship:

1. _____
   _____

2. _____
   _____

3. _____
   _____

In 1 Chronicles we read of what happened when the ark of the covenant came back to Jerusalem:

> "So all Israel brought up the ark of the covenant of the Lord with shouts, with the sounding of rams' horns and trumpets, and of cymbals, and the playing of lyres and harps." (1 Chronicles 15:28)

Music played an important role in the worship festivities.

Psalm 150 is perhaps one of the most musical psalms, and the one often quoted by drummers who are having a tough time with the more senior members of the congregation! In all these issues it is the aim that is most important. The aim of music should always be to honour God, for as David says,

> "Come let us sing for joy to the Lord; let us shout aloud to the Rock of our salvation. Let us come before him with thanksgiving and extol him with music and song." (Psalm 95:1,2)

Admittedly, references to music in the New Testament are more difficult to find, but you cannot build an argument from silence! This has been used by some to suggest that we need to question the use of music in our churches today.

However, I find it fascinating to recognise that when the birth of Jesus was announced, God used a praise gathering of angels and we are told that when Jesus comes a second time, "the trumpet shall sound" (1 Corinthians 15:52). I have more than a shrewd suspicion that heaven is going to be filled with music and praise!

LET'S BE QUIET

What a noisy world we live in. From the moment we wake to the time we lay our heads on the pillow, we can be surrounded by noise. Some people have become conditioned to noise so that if you give them peace and quiet they become most irritable.

I was once leading a congregation in worship and suggested that we pause for stillness and quiet. I gave no particular instruction on how to use that time and found it quite revealing to note the amount of embarrassment after a couple of minutes.

God's people need to take time to be still. It's a command that He gives: "Be still and know that I am God" (Psalm 46:10) and we must remember that it is so often in quietness that we hear that still, small voice.

KEY QUESTION

Psalm 150 says,

Praise the Lord.
Praise God in his sanctuary; praise him in his mighty heavens.
Praise him for his acts of power; praise him for his surpassing greatness.
Praise him with the sounding of the trumpet, praise him with the harp and lyre,
praise him with tambourine and dancing, praise him with strings and flute, praise him with the clash of cymbals, praise him with resounding cymbals.

Let everything that has breath praise the Lord. Praise the Lord.

This has been described as the "noisy psalm". Does it give us liberty to be more noisy and extrovert in our praise? What, if any, responsibilities are implied in this psalm?

LET'S RAISE OUR HANDS

Physical expression in worship has been for many the pebble to disturb the waters. Those from more traditional backgrounds find it hard to cope with — even if there is a Biblical justification — and it can be seen to pander to the flesh and to give good opportunity to the performers. Perhaps we need to examine the issue more closely, particularly the raising of "holy hands".

Scripture endorses the use of our bodies to glorify the Lord: "Let us lift up our hearts and our hands to God in heaven" (Lamentations 3:41); "I will praise you as long as I live, and in your name I will lift up my hands" (Psalm 63:4). But raising hands always has to be a response of the heart and not merely a standard practice when we come together for worship.

Hands outstretched to God affirm the truth that we sing, indicate the direction of our praise and can symbolise that abandonment to the Lord as we recognise His right to own our lives.

I often encourage people to hold their hands open in an attitude of waiting to receive from God — cupped hands, ready and expectant to take what God has to say and give as part of worship.

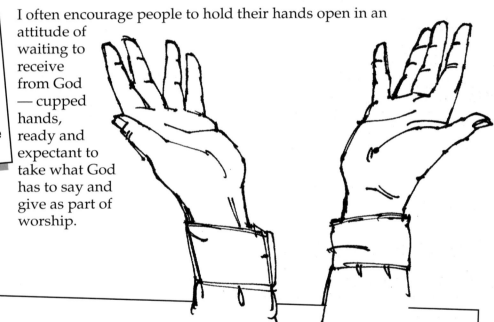

KEY QUESTION

Can you think of times in the Bible when God spoke in the quietness, or when He used stillness to emphasise His sovereignty?

Now list any times when you have been particularly aware of God speaking to you. Ask yourself how you set out to listen to God, and compare your experience with the Bible incidents you have chosen.

THINK . . .

What behaviour is a distraction in worship? Where should the line be drawn in the use of physical expression and bodily movement in our praise?

_____

_____

_____

_____

Take a closer look at Psalm 24. The psalmist asks the question, "Who may ascend the hill of the Lord? Who may stand in his holy place?" and the response comes, "He who has clean hands and a pure heart, who does not lift up his soul to an idol or swear by what is false" (Psalm 24:3,4). To stand in the holy presence of God necessitates having hands that are clean and a heart that is pure.

We shall say more about our preparation for worship a little later, but there is a responsibility involved in the raising of our hands in worship. They must be clean — and not just in terms of physical grime!

However, there is something wonderfully emphatic when a person, whose lifestyle is consistent with Scripture, exalts the Lord with clean hands raised in adoration and appreciation of His goodness.

PEACE — BE STILL!!

One of the "in" topics today is stress — probably because it affects a great proportion of our population. It is certainly prevalent in the Christian Church where many seemed destined on a course for blow-up and burn-out! Stillness, peace and pressure control seem to be increasingly more elusive!

I wonder if you are the kind of person who is prone to allow pressure to cause stress and ill health in your life? Listening to sermons on stillness or doing exercises on meditation will never achieve anything unless we are prepared to be honest and identify the kind of person that we are, and to do something about easing the pressure in our lives. If we don't choose to ease up God often uses alternative methods!

One other note of caution — Christians have a habit of over-spiritualising stress instead of dealing with it. Hence the excuse; "Yes, I'm busy and I find it difficult to be still — but that's just me and may be 'the cross' I have to carry!!" I find no support for this excuse in Scripture and it has no credibility in the light of the fact that God calls us to be good stewards of our time and human resources!

GIVING GOD OUR TIME

There are 168 hours in each week! I wonder if you have ever considered how you use them? Make a list of the activities that predominate your life throughout the week — eating, sleeping, studying, relaxing, working, travelling, serving the Lord, time with family, watching TV, etc.

ACTIVITY

NUMBER OF HOURS PER WEEK

_____   _____

_____   _____

_____   _____

_____   _____

_____   _____

_____   _____

_____   _____

_____   _____

_____   _____

_____

1. Consider the amount of time you give to God. Is this a fair proportion?

2. Is it worth considering tithing time? Should we be giving one tenth of our time to the Lord for Him to use?

GIVING GOD OUR MONEY

"Now let's sing 'O God our help in ages past' as we take up the offering!! . . . "

Have you noticed how easily and indeed how often, the giving of monetary gifts is divorced from the main flow of worship when we come together in our fellowships? It's almost like an interlude — some would even say an inconvenience — that has to be accommodated, because without financial help, the drains would never be cleaned out and the roof would never get repaired!

After all is said and done, giving money to the church can be a great conscience reliever and is a wonderful way to express one's love for our fellow neighbour! What a tragedy that many seem to hold on to this idea and live in the false hope that financial giving itself might make them a better person in the eyes of God.

We need to start at the beginning. God made the heaven and the earth and put man in charge of it. Man was to be a good steward and to treat the earth well.

All that we have belongs to God. We don't own anything and while we are here on this earth, our responsibility is to be a good steward of the planet and its resources. That includes the money and goods that may or may not accrue for each of us. Furthermore, the Word of God is very clear about our responsibilities in this area.

The Hebrew tradition was to tithe. This meant that one tenth of all possessions would be given each year to God, and over and above this, further offerings would be made. When we turn to the New Testament, there are many references that endorse God's attitude towards possessions and again it becomes abundantly clear that God loves us to give back to Him that which He has primarily supplied.

"God loves a cheerful giver" — so says 2 Corinthians 9:7. So why is it that in a spirit of meanness we rummage around in the recesses of our pockets to find the smallest coin that we can slip unobtrusively onto the offering plate as it is passed around the congregation?

Giving gifts to God is all part of worship and should be fully integrated into our services as a vital component of presenting our sacrifice of praise. Sacrificial giving should be an important element of our worship. Even though the Hebrew traditions are perhaps in the past, the principle of tithing is healthy when applied to today's church. Surely 10% is the *least* we can give in the light of a God who gave us 100% of what He had!

> " 'Bring the whole tithe into the store-house, that there may be food in my house. Test me in this,' says the Lord Almighty, 'and see if I will not throw open the floodgates of heaven and pour out so much blessing that you will not have room enough for it.' " (Malachi 3:10)

REMEMBER: YOU CAN NEVER OUT-GIVE GOD!!

KEY QUESTION

You are left £10,000 by a rich Aunt who has died. Suggest ways whereby you would use the money! Be honest with yourself — don't try to be super-spiritual with your answers!

WHERE THE MONEY GOES   **AMOUNT**

_____   _____

_____   _____

_____   _____

_____   _____

_____   _____

4 Battle in Worship

To be looking at spiritual warfare in a book on worship might appear strange to people whose understanding of worship primarily embraces hymn singing and church attendance. However, any study of the growth of the early Christian church shows that when God's people raise up the name of Jesus and declare His Kingship the opposition makes itself known!

Someone once said that one of the problems of today's church is that we seem to be committed to making people into "sunbeams" whereas we should be producing soldiers. And although military vocabulary can sound offensive and indeed can be taken to unhelpful extremes, the true church could well be described as being a battleship — where the crew are working together and expect to face the enemy.

Unfortunately, instead we have a few cruise ships around, where God's children prefer to bask in the sunshine and anticipate the joys of what lies over the horizon!

KEY QUESTION

James writes, "Submit yourselves to God. Resist the devil and he will flee from you." (James 4:7)

How do we best resist the devil?

_____

_____

_____

_____

Paul, in writing to the Ephesians reminds us

> "For our struggle is not against flesh and blood, but against the rulers, against the authorities, against the powers of this dark world and against the spiritual forces of evil in the heavenly realms." (Ephesians 6:12)

Some of us need to take these words seriously. The Christian life is not a "hayride to heaven". It demands commitment to a leader who expects us to stand for what is right and to face the devil using all the power and authority that is available to us in Christ.

BUT WHAT HAS THIS TO DO WITH WORSHIP?

If our real motive in worship is to delight the Lord, then it is obvious that the devil is not pleased when Christ is exalted. His reaction and strategy is to undermine our faith in every possible way — by sowing seeds of doubt and by enticing and entangling the Christian with sin.

In short, he determines to cause maximum confusion, chaos and disruption. Of course his power is limited, but he does have influence, and that is why Paul went to great lengths to warn the early Christians of what to expect.

That's the bad news! The good news is that because Jesus conquered the devil and evil when He died on the cross and rose again, so that victory is also ours when we put our faith and trust in Him. Again Paul reminds us, "We are more than conquerors through him who loved us." (Romans 8:37)

And in our worship, as we exalt the Lord and lift up His name, declaring His victory, sovereignty and Kingship, so we declare to the opposition that they are defeated. There is power in praise, and because the devil knows that he has no ultimate victory, when we exalt Christ it reminds him that he has no authority over us. Praise and worship are effective missiles to launch at the enemy!

Again, we need to fully understand the implications here. If our praise merely comes from our lips, not our hearts and lives, that has no effect whatsoever in threatening the devil's devices. But praise that is endorsed by heartfelt worship and a godly life strikes at the core of all that Satan would throw at us, and his "flaming arrows" (Ephesians 6:16) can quickly be extinguished.

Let's not forget that the church is described as being militant *and* triumphant. Militant on earth as we engage in holy warfare, and triumphant — not only on earth but in heaven — where the sword will be exchanged for the palm of victory. What a tragedy that we often get that the wrong way round. But maybe that is because it's easier to be a sunbeam than a soldier!

There are some interesting examples in Scripture of the power in praise. In one New Testament story Paul and Silas are thrown into prison after they had ministered to a girl who was possessed by an evil spirit. Here they were in direct confrontation with the powers of darkness and indeed suffered as a result. They were severely flogged and thrown into prison.

FIGHTING THE FIGHT

Satan prowls around like a roaring lion to undermine God's plans for His people. He wages a tactical war.

1. *He occupies our mind.*
2. *He causes confusion.*
3. *He creates diversions.*
4. *He sows doubt.*
5. *He encourages error.*

But there is always an antidote to his strategy. Look at the following verses. Fit the most appropriate antidote to each tactic listed above and explain why.

Psalm 62:8;
Romans 8:38;
Ephesians 6:17;
John 14:6;
Psalm 32:8

Antidotes

1. _____
2. _____
3. _____
4. _____
5. _____

But Paul and Silas believed in the power of praise, and instead of feeling very sorry for themselves, they began to give thanks to the Lord, singing hymns and psalms. And then, it all happened . . .

Look up Acts 16:25, 26 and express what happened in your own words:

_____

_____

_____

_____

CONSIDER

"To appreciate peace you have to have had experience of war." Discuss.

It caused quite a stir. So much so that the frightened jailer was about to take his own life because he thought that the prisoners had escaped. But Paul and Silas spoke to him, and ultimately led him and his family to the Lord. There is real spiritual power in praise, and here we have a fine example of God's sovereign intervention in a very difficult situation.

But don't assume that whenever we are in trouble that a few bars of "Thine Be The Glory" will see us through! Their praise in prison was only the expression of lives that worshipped God, and on this occasion, God moved in great power. He does do that today of course. I've known people be healed in worship, but equally I've seen sick people untouched by the power of God. Remember, He is sovereign and we can't dictate to Him as to what He should do. That's not our aim in praising Him.

I am also fond of the Old Testament story about the fall of Jericho (Joshua 5 & 6). The Lord gave specific instructions to Joshua as to how the city would be taken; He requested that the Israelites should march around the city for six days with seven priests carrying the trumpets of rams' horns in front of the ark. On the seventh day, the priests were instructed to blow the trumpets, the people told to shout and then the walls of the city would collapse — and that's exactly what happened. It was one of the most successful open air witnesses of all time and a wonderful example of God moving in power. Now I realise it might be dangerous to draw too much out of this story, but one thing is certain, God honoured obedience. I wouldn't be surprised if that shout was the Hebrew equivalent of "Praise the Lord"!

God reminds us of His authority and power that He wants us to use. Can you think of some verses of Scripture that support this statement?

1. _____
   _____

2. _____
   _____

3. _____
   _____

TACTICAL WARFARE

In our understanding of spiritual warfare we need to be specific as to the ways in which Satan operates. Peter writes,

> "Your enemy the devil prowls around like a roaring lion looking for someone to devour." (1 Peter 5:8)

Just as a lion stalks its prey, Satan looks for that opportunity in our lives that he can use for his own end.

So often it is when we have experienced great encouragement and blessing — maybe in our witness, seeing people come to Christ or watching God move in a particular situation — and then the difficulty comes or tragedy strikes. Now I don't think we can blame the devil for everything, but he is certainly clever in timing how he mounts his attacks.

PERSONAL TESTIMONY

It had been one of our best missions, and in my home town. Many young people had come to know Christ and even the local newspapers carried stories about the change in peoples' lives.

Two months later, while travelling back home, I was involved in a terrible car accident and two people were killed. I had not been driving erratically, neither had I been driving fast. In fact, at the subsequent inquest when a verdict of accidental death was reached, the coroner indicated that there was a mystery concerning why the accident actually happened. There seemed to be no real human explanation.

I can't describe how I felt during that time, but Satan had played a master stroke. The same newspapers carried a different story, this time about a "death-car preacher" and it was a very difficult time.

PRAISE THE LORD
(Brown Bannister/Mike Hudson/Kenwood Music)

When you're up against a struggle
That shatters all your dreams
And your hopes have been cruelly crushed by Satan's manifested schemes
And you feel the urge within you to submit to earthly fear
Don't let the faith you're standing on seem to disappear

Chorus
Praise the Lord, God can work through those who praise Him
Praise the Lord — for our God inhabits praise
Praise the Lord — for the chains that seem to bind you
Serve only to remind you that they fall
Powerless behind you when you praise Him.

Now Satan is a liar and he wants to make us think
We are paupers, when he knows himself we are children of the King
So lift that mighty shield of faith for the battle must be won
We know that Jesus Christ is risen
So the work's already done.

Friends prayed, and I clung onto a faith that was very weak and fragile.

With the passage of time, God brought me through — scarred, yes and full of questions which are still unanswered. But I do now recognise how Satan launches his attacks. However, he always overplays his hand, and it was through this tragedy that others came to know Christ . . . which is why I know:

> "that neither life nor death, neither angels nor demons, neither the present nor the future, nor any powers, neither height nor depth, nor anything else in all creation, will be able to separate us from the love of God that is in Christ Jesus our Lord."
> (Romans 8:38–39)

The devil always overplays his hand! And in the darkest circumstances, God can fulfil His purposes. Identify the difficult times in your own life when you have been under attack. Share this experience (if you are able) with someone.

What did God teach you in that situation — about Himself and about you?

_____

_____

_____

_____

_____

TO SUCCEED IN BATTLE

1. We must recognise and believe that we are on the victory side, and live our lives accordingly. When we are oppressed or under attack, we need to call upon the Lord to help us. Just as Jesus commanded Satan to leave Him when He was in the wilderness, so we are able to use Christ's authority to rebuke the devil. Unfortunately we sometimes take the line of "why pray when you can panic?" Let's remember, Jesus has given us power that He wants us to use to His glory.

2. We must wear the armour of God (Ephesians 6:10–18). This is given to us for our protection. A friend of mine once told me how, when he begins the day, he mentions each piece of armour before the Lord, and puts on the whole armour of God before he leaves the house. Never forget the helmet! Our thought life is an easy target, but when the helmet of salvation covers the head, so Christ is able to protect our minds from impurity and uncleanliness.

3. We must lift high the name of Jesus. The Bible reminds us that there is power in His name, and one day "that at the name of Jesus every knee should bow, . . . and every tongue confess that Jesus Christ is Lord" (Philippians 2:10). James tells us that the "demons believe there is one God — and shudder" (James 2:19) and in our worship, we must use the name of Jesus to bring a counter attack in spiritual warfare. Charles Wesley expressed it so well,

> "Jesus, the name high over all, in hell or earth or sky;
> Angels and men before it fall and demons fear and fly."

4. We must apply the blood of Christ . . . a rather strange expression perhaps, but this takes us to the root of understanding why we have power available to us to use in spiritual warfare. When Jesus died, His blood was shed so that we could receive God's forgiveness for sin. Jesus had to allow His life to be taken, so that He could truly be our Saviour. The blood of Christ is the absolute guarantee of all that God has promised to do in us and for us.

Some critics of the gospel declare that Christians have a morbid curiosity about the blood of Christ; the truth is that without the shedding of blood, there could be no forgiveness, and without forgiveness, there could never be victory.

KEY QUESTION

Study Ephesians 6:10-18

1. Identify the armour of God.

2. How does each piece of the armour protect us or provide a resource for us to use?

Notice we are not given any armour to cover our backs. Should that be something we do for each other as part of fellowship and love for each other?

How should this be done, practically?

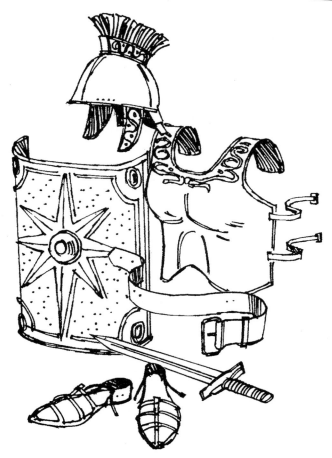

33

Much is said and done today to discredit the church. Unbelievers consider it to be out of date, and out of touch with reality. Even some within the Christian family are quick to underline its faults and failings, rather than highlight the strengths. Again, it must be said that there is no perfect church; if there was then I, for one, would need to keep clear because it would become imperfect the moment my shadow darkened the doorway!

The church is the visible expression of the body of Christ here on earth. Even with its faults and failings, it is the instrument that God chooses to use to fulfil His purposes in worship, mission and evangelism.

Jesus started it when He took His disciples to Caesarea Philippi and after Peter's confession of faith declared, "on this rock I will build my church" (Matthew 16:18). It is when we confess Christ with our lips and honour Him with our lives that we become members of the body of Christ, grafted into the fastest growing organisation in the whole world! Does that surprise you? Well, it's true, because the church is the only organisation that never loses a member through death!

It would be wrong to gloss over many of the problems that exist at local church level, but many of these are individually orientated. We may want to criticise the worship services, the songs, the music, the leadership, etc., but we should first examine our own hearts to see if the root of the problem is within ourselves.

When we come together to worship, how well have we prepared ourselves? Are we expecting to meet the Lord as we come into His house? We need to give honest answers to these questions.

PREPARATION FOR WORSHIP

1. Be determined. Let's not fall into the trap of thinking that worship comes easily. In the pace of life today, it becomes increasingly difficult to give quality time to worshipping God. We have to become very disciplined — even when we are in the church — to make sure that we achieve our goals.

But, we are in good company! The Psalmist David used great effort at times to stir up his spirit into worship. In Psalm 108 he encourages himself to praise the Lord. He is taking himself by the scruff of the neck and applying discipline of heart and mind:

"My heart is steadfast, O God;
I *will* sing and make music with all my soul.
Awake, harp and lyre!
I *will* awaken the dawn.
I *will* praise You, O Lord, among the nations;
I *will* sing of You among the peoples." `(Psalm 108:1–3)

When you don't feel like praising, or when you're depressed or under pressure, that's when you need to do the same as David did. When we are determined, God meets us in our efforts and enables our spirits to rise up. There is power in praise.

2. Be enthusiastic. How often do we lose heart because it's a case of the morning after the night before? Maybe you're tired because of a late Saturday night, or the baby woke you at 4:00 am, or financial pressures kept you tossing and turning. There may be countless reasons, and such experiences bring tiredness that undermines enthusiasm. God deserves more than the dregs when we worship Him and as we lift our hearts in praise, we need to encourage an enthusiastic response to His love and goodness.

3. Be honest. There are, of course, times when we legitimately find it difficult to praise God. Maybe the heat of the battle has become too great. Perhaps something has happened to cause great sadness and we have a heavy heart. Praise is the last thing we feel like doing. God needs to know about that — even in our worship.

The tendency might be to opt out or switch off, but instead we need to be honest before God and confess our need and our difficulty in worship — even if this means our being still when everyone else is getting excited.

My experience is that God meets us in that situation, and although He may not plant a huge smile upon our faces, He is able to minister to our hurts, and inspire us with renewed power and encouragement if we are honest and real before Him. Let's not assume that valid worship can only come from "mountain-top" experiences! Valley experiences can teach us so much more about God and give Him greater opportunity to minister into our lives.

A little while ago now, I experienced a trauma that I find very painful to bring back into my memory. It was a deep valley but, now, some years on, I would be prepared to admit that through it all God taught me more about Himself than ever before. I would have preferred to have learnt some other way, but being honest about my doubt, anger and frustration helped me to appreciate God's constancy and unchanging nature. That ultimately led me into new depths of praise and heights of expression.

"The Lord is my shepherd, I shall not be in want. He makes me lie down in green pastures, he leads me beside quiet waters, he restores my soul. He guides me in paths of righteousness for his name's sake. Even though I walk through the valley of the shadow of death, I will fear no evil, for you are with me; your rod and your staff, they comfort me. You prepare a table before me in the presence of my enemies. You anoint my head with oil; my cup overflows. Surely goodness and love will follow me all the days of my life, and I will dwell in the house of the Lord for ever."
(Psalm 23)

Read through Psalm 23 and identify how this Psalm emphasises the importance of honesty in worship.

1. Underline the phrases that have been proved true and relevant, then write alongside a brief comment — perhaps a year date or situation or place or name — which will remind you of worship in valley experiences.

2. Now turn this Psalm into a personal prayer and worship time — and as you read it aloud add in your comments: e.g. "He restores my soul" — I worship You, Lord, for Your faithfulness, for the way You met me and helped me when things were tough/When I was unemployed, etc.

4. Be thankful. How easy it is to take God, and all that He gives us, for granted! The beauty of the earth, the miracle of creation, the provision of food and clothing, the constancy of His love. Sometimes we need to stop and remind ourselves of these things and thank Him for His provision and faithfulness.

Paul encourages us to "give thanks in all circumstances" (1 Thessalonians 5:18). Of course, we find that very difficult, but that is where God is wanting to pour His blessing and encouragement into our lives.

5. Be consistent. I make no apology for reiterating what I have stressed in previous sections. Worship is not just a performance on a Sunday morning; it is a way of life.

I've always been fascinated with what Paul wrote to the Corinthians when he said, "I will pray with my spirit, but I will also pray with my mind; I will sing with my spirit, but I will also sing with my mind"(1 Corinthians 14:15). When we finish our corporate worship, that same emphasis should not leave us as we leave the church. We carry that attitude in all that we do, the way we talk to people, our performance at work, our willingness to serve, etc. These are all ways whereby we show a consistency in our worship.

The mind is the centre of behaviour; what enters our minds is translated into behaviour patterns which is exactly why Paul recognises the potential of applying our minds to the ongoing responsibility of worship.

6. Be clean. You would not be greatly blessed if someone arrived at your home and trampled dirt and grime all over your clean dining room carpet! Guests with dirty shoes normally wipe their feet before they enter a house, and in extreme cases might even suggest they remove their shoes!

How many of us rush into the Lord's presence and find ourselves singing the first hymn or song without confessing our sin and unworthiness? We must ask God to forgive us and clean us up in preparation for what is about to take place?

How many of us harbour grudges as we worship, allowing bitterness to gnaw away in our minds? Or remember literature or something we saw on television that was and is not helpful? We need to confess that before worship so that we come with clean hands and pure hearts.

7. Be thoughtful. When you meet up with friends you may have a great desire to discuss the football scores or Mrs Jones' intestinal operation! Resist the temptation to get involved in thoughtful — or thoughtless — conversation until the priority of worship is accomplished.

When I am leading worship I will often encourage a congregation to meditate on a verse of Scripture as they enter the presence of the Lord, or to pray quietly and ask for God's help in clearing away all the preoccupations and concerns of life as we prepare for worship. Even praying that God will bless others, and indeed those leading the worship, can be a wonderful way of causing us to look out from ourselves as we make preparation to give our best to the Lord.

Psalm 37 was written towards the end of David's life. As he looked back on the wealth of his experience — in good times and bad — he drew attention to many of the things he had learned and appreciated about God.

He expresses them in this psalm in a manner that harnesses his spirit and stirs himself to take hold of basic truths; they are written as commands. Can you identify them?
(Clue: there are six in the first nine verses!)

1 _____

2 _____

3 _____

4 _____

5 _____

6 _____

7 _____

8 _____

Be . . .
Which of these nine "Be's" is God speaking to you about?

_____

_____

How will you put this into action?

_____

_____

8. Be attentive. When God made us, He gave us twice as many ears as mouths. We need to listen for God to speak to us as we worship — maybe in the stillness, maybe through the preacher, maybe through someone else, or through a song — certainly through the Word. Be attentive!

9. Be decisive. Having explained the strong relationship between worship and lifestyle, I always think it wise to ask oneself at the end of a worship experience what God has said and what needs to be done to follow through in a spirit of obedience.

It's all too easy to drift in and out of worship and be unchanged. Ideally, time spent with God can only remind us of His holiness and majesty, and subsequently our failure and simple nature. Leaving His presence should be accompanied by a renewed determination to make changes so that we become more Christlike in our day to day lives.

FELLOWSHIP IN WORSHIP

I'm not sure whether it is permissible to have a favourite book in the Bible. All Scripture is given by the inspiration of God and, to that end, one book is as important as the next. But if I was really pushed, I would confess that my favourite is the Acts of the Apostles.

It's an insight into what happens when God takes ordinary people, fills them with Himself and enables them to become extraordinary for Him. One of the undergirding principles of the Acts, is that God can greatly use men and women in fellowship with each other, and I think it is that which excites me the most.

In Acts 1 we read of a tremendous prayer meeting. One hundred and twenty people met for ten days to pray together and seek the Lord's face in praise, worship and adoration.

Can you imagine the sense of expectation there? No wonder that the Holy Spirit came in such power a little later. It's worth noticing how God used people when they came together with the express purpose of honouring Him.

These folk were so filled with the power of God that some of the people in the street began to question if they were drunk. Such was the effect of God's Spirit on the Christians' lives that it had an astounding impact on ordinary people. They were amazed at what they saw and heard from their lips. After Peter had preached, over 3,000 people were added to the church.

Never underestimate the power of corporate praise and worship. It can be a most useful tool in the communication of the Gospel and the reality of God.

And maybe that's why the devil focuses much of his activity on generating squabbles and differences in the church. If he can drive a wedge between worshippers and introduce strife through petty squabbles and arguments, he neutralises our evangelistic enthusiasm.

Often, in our studies of spiritual warfare, we examine how our fight is with the world. That can be a glorious diversion from recognising that the devil prefers to split the ranks from inside. If he can do that successfully, the battle is won even before the fight.

We've all heard that amusing but ironic rhyme, "To dwell above with saints we love, for that will be glory; to dwell below with saints we know, well that's another story." Interestingly enough, whenever the Bible refers to saints, it is always in the plural and even in the one instance when it is used in the singular, the implication is plural: "Greet every saint" (Philippians 4:21, NKJV). God wants us to live in harmony with each other. Yes, He has made us different but that is no excuse for not being united.

KEY QUESTION
Jesus taught extensively on the issue of personal relationships affecting our worship. Read Matthew 5:23–24, 40–42; Matthew 6:14–15; Matthew 7:1–5. What is the importance of this teaching in the development of relationships within the Christian family?

I enjoy listening to an orchestral concert (as frequently as my diary allows). I'm always greatly impressed with the diversity of instruments and the variety of sound that is created. The violinist is scraping the strings, the oboist is blowing through a reed, the percussionist is striking various objects, but the overall sound is beautiful. Why? Because, under the leadership of the conductor and with all eyes on the same music score, the orchestra plays in tune with itself and it creates harmony. What an excellent picture of what Christian fellowship should be like.

God wants us to use our distinctiveness and our various personalities and gifts to create that which honours Him. Not only does it give Him great pleasure, but it has tremendous evangelistic impact. When we love one another, the unbelievers ask all the right questions!

WORSHIP AND THE INDIVIDUAL

If all the words that have been written about how to cultivate a personal walk with the Lord were put end to end, I would not dare to hazard a guess as to how far they would stretch. But if all that has been written was absorbed into the lives of the readers, then our land would be a very different place to inhabit!

I therefore do not want to add too many extra words to that which has already been penned, but at the same time, I want to draw your attention to the importance of developing a deep relationship with the Lord on a personal level.

God has given us enough time to accomplish all that He wants us to do. If we are under pressure because there are not enough hours in the day, that's not God's problem — it's our mismanagement. Look back to section three and read again the material on giving God our time. Tragically, it's when we're under time constraints that our own personal devotions come under attack and so often become squeezed out. We then wonder why we are spiritually powerless and full of doubt. The answer is obvious, but the antidote requires discipline of mind and behaviour. May I suggest the way ahead?

TAKE TIME OUT ...

1. To praise

Develop the habit of recognising the good things God has done, even in a fallen world. Be aware of His grace and boundless love as it is reflected in much of what we see around us — the innocent smile of a child, the helping hand, the beauty of creation. Recognise it too in the more practical aspects of life — food to eat, friendship to enjoy, the gifts of life and health and strength. Take time out to thank God for His goodness.

2. To pray

Some people seem to think that you can only pray first thing in the morning or just before you go to bed at night. This is what I call the duvet mentality! God is eager to listen to us at any time in the day and I try to keep a constant prayer awareness so that I take and make good opportunities to talk to God.

There must always be quality time for prayer, when we apply discipline of mind and give ourselves to praise and bringing our petitions before the Lord. That may be either early in the morning or late in the day. But this quality time also needs to be supplemented by other prayer opportunities.

I sometimes pray driving my car — keeping my eyes open of course — but at least I'm not interrupted by the telephone or other intrusions of people making demands on my time. Don't forget to take time out to pray.

3. To meditate

The psalmist David discovered the secrets of meditation and it's worth underlining their importance here. (The first handbook in this series deals exclusively with this subject — *Getting the Best out of the Bible: A New Look at Biblical Meditation* by Selwyn Hughes.)

As David sat alone on the Judean hills, he meditated on God: on His attributes, on His Word, and David became stronger for it. Meditation inspired his praise and worship and gave him a deeper insight into the riches of heaven. He writes, "I will meditate on all your works and consider all your mighty deeds" (Psalm 77:12).

Take a phrase from Scripture, or a title that Jesus is given, and think on those words. Turn them over in your mind and see what other flashes of light God brings into your understanding as you consider the various facets of meaning in the truth that God gives. Take time to meditate.

THINK ON THESE THINGS

66 Finally, brothers, whatever is true, whatever is noble, whatever is right, whatever is pure, whatever is lovely, whatever is admirable — if anything is excellent or *PRAISEWORTHY* — THINK ABOUT SUCH THINGS. **99**

(Philippians 4:8, capitals mine)

Paul recognised the importance and potential of private meditation. Here is a verse of Scripture that I want you to use so that you can also learn this discipline.

66 Do you not know? Have you not heard? The Lord is the everlasting God, the Creator of the ends of the earth. He will not grow tired or weary, and his understanding no-one can fathom. **99**

(Isaiah 40:28)

1 Read this text slowly to yourself. As you concentrate on these words, how do they affect how you feel about God, yourself and others?

2 Let every word soak into your mind. Visualise the meanings as far as possible.

3 Now, talk to God about what you read. (If doing this study with others — use this as a basis for corporate prayer.) For example — picture the vastness of creation, the rolling oceans, the azure blue sky and then thank God for His power and majesty displayed in His handiwork.

4 Meditate on this verse over the next 24 hours — perhaps when you are walking to work, sitting in a traffic jam (!), during your lunch break, perhaps make it the last thought in your mind before you drift off to sleep at night. If you find it difficult to remember, write the verse on a small card and read it from time to time throughout the day.

6

Lead in Worship

Over the past few years, there has been a growing awareness that leading in worship is more than linking a few hymns, choruses and prayers together just before someone preaches. Spiritual winds of change are blowing through our fellowships.

The emergence of conventions and conferences that are geared to introduce the body to a variety of worship experiences, together with the recent focus on celebration evangelism and praise marches, have all served to encourage a greater appreciation of the ministry of leading in worship.

But of course the responsibilities here are enormous, for the worship leader has to be able to take people close to the heart of God and sense how best to achieve that quality of praise and adoration that is a real blessing to the Lord.

This does raise one very basic question. How do I know whether I'm a worship leader? It would certainly be wrong to assume that just because I can strum a few guitar chords or sing in tune, this qualifies me to lead worship.

I'm a firm believer in testing one's gifts! If you sense you are gifted to lead worship, take the opportunity when it arises and wait to see what happens. Listen to what people say, ask mature leaders for an honest opinion and above all, look for God's blessing amongst the people. It will be very obvious after the passage of time. However, it is worth examining for a few moments the qualifications and qualities necessary to be an effective worship leader.

1. Be worshipful

First and foremost, a worship leader needs to be a worshipper!

There often seems to be some confusion between leading in worship and being a performer or a song leader. The distinction must be made very clear.

There may be a person in the congregation who has great gifts of oratory, plays the guitar "par excellence", has a voice that is only matched by Pavarotti(!), but if that person is not primarily a worshipper, he will not lead people into the Lord's presence. As someone once commented, "Fine performance but you missed the whole point".

2. Be prayerful

"Tell God about the church before you tell the church about God". This is an important perspective that we need to learn. If ministry is to be fruitful, it can never bring lasting blessing unless it is bathed

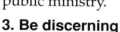

in prayer. All the natural, or indeed spiritual, gifting can never be a substitute for time spent before the Lord seeking His blessing, counsel and help as the leader prepares his heart to minister to God's people.

I shall never forget some advice that I was given by a well-respected leader and indeed a fine preacher. Shortly after my coming into Christian service he said "Never forget these words my boy. What you are in public depends totally upon what you are in private." I have never forgotten those words, hence the emphasis on prayer as we think through the responsibilities of public ministry.

3. Be discerning

Faced with a congregation, how can you sense what God wants to say and what He wants to do? There may be a cross-section of people — some extrovert, others introvert, some wanting to be demonstrative, others wanting to be more reserved. How can you pitch the tenor of praise so as to take people close to the heart of God? This is where the gift of discernment is so useful; that sensitivity to the Spirit's leading that motivates and directs.

4. Be flexible

How easy it would be if, seven days before leading people in worship, it was possible to know which hymns and worship songs were going to be sung, which readings were to be read and what contributions would be made by members of the congregation. "But," you say, "Wait a moment, my fellowship is like that!" Choosing my words carefully, I hesitate to suggest that regimented orthodoxy can kill the vibrancy and spontaneity of worship. If we accept that God is dynamic and the Holy Spirit is "capricious in His working", then we must allow a degree of flexibility so that we can be more adaptable and open to changing emphases.

5. Be prepared

Recently some fellowships have questioned whether it is best to push preparation to one side in order to allow the Holy Spirit to take complete control of their worship time. Therefore the leader who wants to include specific hymns, readings and prayers has often had to cope with the criticism that he may quench the Spirit in his desire to "control" worship.

As is often the case, surely the right perspective is a balance between the two positions. God expects us to be thorough and diligent in our preparation for worship so that we are aware of what material we want to use and where we want to take the people. Built into that strategy however, must be the element of flexibility that we have just discussed.

It is true that rigidity can make sure that God's "frozen chosen" never thaw out, but a sensitive worship leader will be able to discern what God is saying and where He is directing and move the people accordingly — even if that may mean altering a prepared plan. It is probably worth pointing out that the better prepared you are the more flexible you can be.

> **ACT**
>
> Prepare an order of service for family worship next Sunday morning, taking into account all that will be needed in terms of preparation.

6. Be patient

Do not expect the music of heaven after three worship services! Building relationships and bridges between the people, the team (if there is one) and the leader is of paramount importance in leading worship. With all the suspicions, hopes and fears that exist in our fellowships today, this all takes time.

As the congregation's confidence in your leadership ability builds, so they will come to trust you more and will be more eager to follow where you are leading.

The same principle applies if you are working with a team. It takes time to develop that sense of support and encouragement and that ability to know a "oneness" in purpose.

7. Be a leader

Leaders lead, which means that *they take people with them* to wherever they are going! Unfortunately, this is sometimes forgotten and in the excitement of praise and worship, it is possible to leave people behind! The worship leader needs to be able to instil confidence and gently take people forward.

Of course, no-one will never be able to lead farther than he has been himself and this merits careful consideration. The worship leader must be developing and deepening his own relationship with the Lord, and using his experience to gain a maturity and understanding in how to give the best to God.

Jesus once encouraged His disciples to launch out into the deep. That was good advice at the time, and at the risk of being accused of taking words out of context, I would suggest that a worship leader needs to follow the Master's advice — to launch out into deeper water.

Use silence in worship, encourage a congregation to kneel, allow freedom of expression; these may not be the easiest worship styles to encourage, but the effect can be amazing. For fear of being intimidated, a leader can allow worship to become stale and fail to push back some of the traditions that people tend to cling on to for safety's sake!

Of course there will always be those who don't want to be taken anywhere, who are content to maintain the status quo and subscribe to the view that "as it was in the beginning is now and ever shall be!" Such people are likely to find heaven a little uncomfortable!

FROM THEORY TO PRACTICE

I now want to examine how much of this works out in practice. Let's take as an example the situation of a worship leader, working with three or four musicians in an average 60 member church fellowship. Of course every church situation is different, but whether your church relies on you and your guitar, or a leader with an orchestra, or simply you plus a pianist and an enthusiastic organist, there are some useful ideas to learn that are worth learning and applying. We look at some basic principles.

THINK . . .

What can we learn from the traditions of the past? How do these things prepare us for what God wants to do in and through us?

_____

_____

_____

_____

_____

44

1. Keep church leadership informed!

This may sound sensible, but it is amazing how some people really can assume too much. If the minister or vicar is apprehensive about expanding the worship and introducing a leadership team, do make sure that you listen to what he has to say, and try to understand what is causing his apprehension. Perhaps he has previously had a bad experience of musicians — maybe too loud or too performance orientated — or he may have other concerns. Remember the importance of listening to others and attempting to understand someone else's concerns.

Work hard at dovetailing the content of the worship into the theme of the service. Discover what the sermon is to be based on, and try to gear some of the worship to accentuate the theme. Learn to work together, because worship can be a wonderful preparation for God to speak into people's lives through a challenging exposition of His Word.

2. Develop a servant attitude

Worship leaders should be *servants first and leaders second*. Why do I say this? Because I have seen it happen so many times where the person "up front" is working to a fixed agenda. He may be determined to use certain songs, or determined to make people do certain things and determined to make sure that he is in control. This spirit of determination results in catastrophe. There can be embarrassment amongst the people, confusion in the worship, reluctance to participate and the fear of being involved.

The worship leader must have a servant heart and aim to develop a servant spirit. He is there to serve the Lord and to serve the people and not to achieve his own ambitions by serving himself.

Paul's words in 2 Corinthians 4:5 are salutary here. Write them down as a reminder:

_____

_____

_____

3. Be thorough in preparation

Knowing ten songs and owning a guitar is no qualification for being a good worship leader! Yet there are worship teams operating in churches around the country that spend precious little time in rehearsing and indeed praying together. There is really no short-cut to hard work — even in the ministry.

If you want to see God at work in the lives of the people and Him being exalted in their midst, then you have to choose to apply body, mind and spirit to what God has called you to do. Regular rehearsals, practising songs, being familiar with music, and learning words all are part of being efficient in service.

KEY QUESTION

When Paul wrote to the Corinthians, he asked that worship should be conducted in an orderly way. He concludes his request by saying,

   "But everything should be done in a fitting and orderly way."
   (1 Corinthians 14:40)

From your own experience, where does disorder creep into worship? How can the quality of worship be best protected?

_____

_____

_____

_____

_____

_____

_____

_____

_____

It is worth spending time on developing the "art" of linking material. How often has the flow of praise been interrupted by some insensitive character fumbling with a hymn book trying to announce the next song and at the same time forgetting the number? He may then forget the correct musical key, and before long chaos reigns supreme!

Whereas we shouldn't aim to become "slick" in our presentation, we need to take care lest our presentation methods degenerate and become sloppy. It is also worth encouraging members of the worship team to look as if they are enjoying their ministry. If people are nervous about playing the right notes or totally absorbed in the music this can cause some folks to sing with their mouths closed! Which certainly does not encourage others as they try to enter into a spirit of praise.

4. Check the sound system

Public address systems are all too often the minister's nightmare! We've all known it happen: high pitched whistles, radio microphones picking up instructions for the local taxi firm, the sound coming out as inaudible mutterings at the back of the church and loud bumblings at the front!

There is no short-cut to making sure that the P.A. system is good, that it is well installed and correctly used and maintained. This demands time, effort and patience, but is worth *all* the investment because if people can't hear properly it is worth questioning the validity of what you are doing.

5. Encourage the people

The ministry of encouragement is probably the most underrated gift in Christian service today. Yet it is one of the most useful gifts if you are going to steer people into a greater understanding of worshipping God.

We've mentioned earlier the diversity of gift and personality that one finds in a fellowship, and the leader has to take all of these on board. If some people are reluctant to use new material, then this has to be handled sensitively; and give them great encouragement when new ideas are introduced.

Make sure that you teach thoroughly and encourage profusely. Encourage people to relax in the presence of God and to open up to Him. Encourage people to be more enthusiastic; don't tell them that they are hopeless! They will only dig their heels in further and become more hardened and set in their ways.

6. Be open to criticism

Anyone who is involved in Christian leadership must be prepared to handle criticism. It may be difficult, hurtful or even misdirected, but it is all part of the blessings and joys of standing on the front line.

Listen carefully to what is said. Don't immediately be on the defensive. Evaluate the content of criticism, pray through it — maybe with another member of the leadership team — and if appropriate, take whatever action is necessary. But at all costs — keep on going unless you really do have flashing red lights.

7. Share the responsibility

Good leaders can be desperately bad at delegating! With all the responsibility that is heaped upon someone, it may seem easier to take the line of least resistance when it comes to getting things done. As a result, the few are grossly overworked.

Try to share the practical responsibilities — setting up the amplification, writing up the acetates, packing gear away etc. During the ministry, try to involve others in reading, introducing songs, leading prayers and contributing to the worship. It is often well worth the risk.

Note down which of these seven points you need to give more attention to:

_____

_____

How will you seek to do this?

_____

_____

_____

"The Danish philosopher Kierkegaard compared worship to a dramatic production.

> 'In worship, it often seems as though the worship leader is the actor and God is the prompter, whispering into his ear, telling him what to do next. The congregation listen and, at the end, they "applaud" if they like the way he's led worship, or throw things if they don't!'

"But Kierkegaard said that back to front. In reality, God is the audience, the congregation are the actors and the person leading worship is the prompter, simply keeping the production going.

"So when we come together to worship, we come waiting to please God alone, offering to Him our very best."[1]

POSTSCRIPT

Our study of worship has led us over much biblical territory. How fitting, then, that we should conclude it at the threshold of the Temple. There within we glimpse the prophet Isaiah as he receives, in Isaiah chapter six, his dazzling vision of the glory of God.

If ever there was proof that heart worship stimulates action and vision — here we have it! Isaiah's view of the Lord, "high and exalted", exuding power and majestic presence, reminds him of his weakness and failure. "Woe to me," he cries, "I am ruined! For I am a man of unclean lips, and I live among a people of unclean lips, and my eyes have seen the King, the Lord Almighty" (v.5).

And then God touches him, takes away his guilt and, through cleansing and forgiveness, commissions him into service. "Whom shall I send?" says the Lord of Hosts. "Here am I," says Isaiah, "Send me" (vv. 8–9).

What a wonderful seal on the effectiveness of worship. Isaiah's is a heart after God that appreciates His sovereignty, acknowledges his own failure, is open to cleansing and is available for service. And yet this is God's purpose today for each one of us. May the insights in these pages as to what constitutes worship launch many, you and I included, into greater areas of active service and mission.

REFERENCES

CHAPTER ONE

1. A.W. Tozer, *Worship: The Missing Jewel of the Evangelical Church* (Christian Publications Inc., Pennsylvania, 1979; distributed in UK by STL)

2. H.M. Carson, *Hallelujah! Christian Worship*, p. 11 (Evangelical Press, 1980)

3. H.M. Carson, as above, pp. 20–21.

4. C. Brown, *New International Dictionary of the New Testament* (Paternoster Press, 1975)

5. Graham Kendrick, *Worship*, pp. 23–24 (Kingsway, 1984)

CHAPTER TWO

1. R.T. Kendall, *Worshipping God*, p. 21 (Hodder & Stoughton, 1989)

CHAPTER THREE

1. John Blanchard, *Pop Goes the Gospel* (Evangelical Press, 1983, 1989)

CHAPTER SIX

1. N. Mercer & S. Gaukroger, *Frogs in Cream*, p.123 (Scripture Union, 1990)

FURTHER READING

R.T. Kendall, *Worshipping God*, Hodder & Stoughton, 1989

Graham Kendrick, *Worship*, Kingsway, 1984

Selwyn Hughes, *Getting the Best out of the Bible*, CWR, 1989

Herbert Carson, *Hallelujah! Christian Worship*, Evangelical Press, 1980

David Hall, *Dirty Hands*, Kingsway, 1986